LIFE LESSONS FR...
WHO FACED CANCER

Live Full Throttle

To Hanna —
I'm so glad you're
in my life. Godspeed —
Glenn
March 2012

For those
who helped me
re-launch
my life.

You know who
you are.

I love you.

With Profound Appreciation

This work would not exist without the generosity of those who shared their stories with me. If my book succeeds in its mission, others will share my gratitude for their selflessness.

Matt for continuing to carry the torch.

Carter and **Tristan** for making me stronger.

Charles, **David**, **Kereshmeh** and **Matt** for the financial backing.

Catherine, **Dottie** and **Courtney** for your artistic sustenance.

JJ for putting me up on the pegs.

Andy for your wise counsel.

Jim and **Gloria** for life itself.

Be generous in prosperity, and thankful in adversity.

Be worthy of the trust of thy neighbor, and look

upon him with a bright and friendly face.

Be a treasure to the poor, an admonisher to the rich, an answerer of

the cry of the needy, a preserver of the sanctity of thy pledge.

Be fair in thy judgment, and guarded in thy speech.

Be unjust to no man, and show all meekness to all men.

Be as a lamp unto them that walk in darkness, a joy to the sorrowful, a sea for the

thirsty, a haven for the distressed, an upholder and defender of the victim of oppression.

Let integrity and uprightness distinguish all thine acts.

Be a home for the stranger, a balm to the suffering, a tower of strength for the fugitive.

Be eyes to the blind, and a guiding light unto the feet of the erring.

Be an ornament to the countenance of truth, a crown to the brow of fidelity,

a pillar of the temple of righteousness, a breath of life to the body of mankind,

an ensign of the hosts of justice, a luminary above the horizon of virtue, a

dew to the soil of the human heart, an ark on the ocean of knowledge, a sun

in the heaven of bounty, a gem on the diadem of wisdom, a shining light in

the firmament of thy generation, a fruit upon the tree of humility.

~ Gleanings From the Writings of Bahá'u'lláh

Live Full Throttle

Table of Contents

Introduction

The Eight Lessons

Afterword

Live Full Throttle

This book is like an unexpected food to taste buds. Suspend your expectations as you explore, and let yourself contemplate, this memoir and photo essay hybrid that is inspired by the soulful people and places I've encountered as a long-distance motorcyclist for breast cancer causes.

These encounters taught me a great deal about myself and through these stories, pictures and suggested exercises, I hope you will learn about yourself too.

If you choose to flip through the photos, skim the exercises and call it a day, you'll likely forgo the depth of experience I had planned for you when I wrote the book. Plus, you'll never know where I came by these images of people on pink-festooned motorcycles. You might even think you're looking at a bawdy spree when you see pictures of women and men sporting decorated bras atop their street clothes, heads and cowboy hats.

In July 2011, I joined about 50 other motorcyclists from the United States and Canada in Shell, Wyoming (population 50) for a weekend of fundraising for breast cancer research. Photographer Christina Shook, author of *Chicks on Bikes,*

brought her camera equipment to help me document the event. You hold in your hands the product of our collaboration. Friends and I supplemented Christina's photos with other shots from my journey as needed.

The area near the Bighorn National Forest is home to fewer than 4 people per square mile (Charlotte, North Carolina, where I live, is more than 1,700). After a weekend at the Antler Inn in Shell, we motorcyclists, along with a local population of about 1,800, raised $15,000.

I know—it's phenomenal.

Most of the fundraising activities took place outside the Antler Inn in Shell, where we danced to a DJ's playlist and the locals introduced us to Wyoming deep-fried pitchfork steak and other regional dishes.

That answers the question of where most of the photos came from and what people are doing in them, but the discerning reader is also wondering how this group of motorcyclists bound together and why a tiny population in the middle of nowhere is so generous to the breast cancer cause.

WYOMING DEEP-FRIED PITCHFORK STEAK
IS CRISPY ON THE OUTSIDE, TENDER ON THE INSIDE.

THEY DECIDED TO
RIDE FOR BREAST
CANCER SINCE ONE
OF THE GROUP'S
MEMBERS WAS
IN TREATMENT
AT THE TIME.

GOING WITH "THE FLO"

You've probably danced in a Conga line. Someone starts the line with a friend, holding onto their waist from behind and others join in and drop off as the Conga line snakes around the room. The motorcycle Conga ride that Tannis Florence "Flo" Fuhr and her Women Who Ride Rock (WWRR) group operates on the same concept, but instead of dancing on a ballroom floor, we dance across the continent on our motorcycles, raising money for breast cancer research. Start where you are, go as far as you'd like, and if you can make it all the way to the rally point in Wyoming, your life will never be the same.

The Conga seeks no corporate sponsors; all riders pay their own expenses. All monies collected go straight to the designated charity. It's about as grassroots and pure-hearted an endeavor as can be imagined.

Flo started traversing the states in 2008 when she bought a motorcycle in Florida and rode it home to British Columbia. WWRR members accompanied her every mile of the journey: she never rode alone. Emboldened by a successful maiden voyage, Flo agreed to take the trip again in 2009 if supporters would help her by dedicating their efforts to a cause. They decided that cause would be breast cancer since one of the group's members was in treatment at the time.

During her 2009 trip, Flo came through the town of Shell with another Canadian rider to gas up and catch a bite to eat at Dirty Annie's. A cashier there was wearing a bandanna and Flo, whose sister died of colon cancer, knew a chemo patient when she saw one. Flo and her riding companion's motorcycles were decorated in pink, they wore pink jewelry and when they opened their mouths those flat-voweled Canadian accents added to their mystique. A local gave them sidelong glances during his meal and afterward said, "I've gotta ask you a question."

Flo was ready for the question—she was accustomed to people asking why she wrapped a pink swim noodle around her headlight to resemble a breast cancer ribbon. She replied, "It's gonna cost ya."

"How much?"

"As much as you want. A quarter, a dollar, a quarter of a million dollars," said Flo, as she proceeded to tell him that they were raising money for breast cancer research.

"I like breasts," said the local, and wrote a check for $30 before suggesting they go down to the Antler Inn to see what kind of fundraising success she could find there.

Before anyone knew it, the owner of the Antler Inn invited the Conga riders to bunk down for the night in a spare bedroom, some of the local men washed and polished the bikes and $400 was raised. They offered to host a fundraising event in 2010 if she would be a part of it and she agreed.

Live Full Throttle

Cancer Strikes

Cancer struck the little Wyoming community in a big way between 2009 and Flo's return in 2010. Three local women, including the one in the bandanna at Dirty Annie's, died of breast cancer, a devastating blow in a community of that size.

Life on the range has never been easy and if you are a cancer patient in Wyoming, the country's least-populous state, your treatment choices are literally few and far between. From Shell, you must travel to Cody, 70 miles away, or seek care at the larger Billings Clinic Cancer Center, 138 miles from home in Montana. When you're getting chemo treatments that far away, you shouldn't drive yourself, which means you and your driver are both losing a day's wages.

Distance is one thing—health insurance is another. Most folks in the Big Horn Basin work the land or support others who do; their occupations don't come with employee benefits like health insurance. One of the men I met in Shell, whose wife is in cancer treatment, is selling his livestock to keep her in care. Talk about eating your seed corn.

When Flo and the other Conga riders came through Shell in 2010, the locals from Shell and neighboring Greybull raised $4000 in a day by auctioning off donated items, including a pony, hair and beards. Flo pledged to them that the Conga would always make a stop in Shell and decided it would be the rally point for the 2011 Conga.

ROADSIDE BARBERSHOP FUNDRAISING

When the Conga comes to Shell, those who want to donate mop tops or mustaches for the cause can either set their price or go to auction for the highest bid from the crowd. One man who auctioned his beard in 2010 let it grow for a full year so that it would generate the largest possible bid in 2011.

I'm told that one of the first things women worry about when they face chemo is hair loss. In some cultures, widows shave their heads and mark time by their hair growth. Then there's Joelle, pictured here. She lost both her husband and his mother to cancer in the year prior to Conga 2011. She voluntarily shaved her hair for a $500 donation. Her ponytail was donated to Locks of Love, which will turn it into a wig for a cancer patient she'll never meet.

Where I Came In

I learned to ride a motorcycle in 2010 and rode my BMW from Charlotte, North Carolina to Bend, Oregon, where I worked on a book project that summer. Before leaving, I looked for a cause I could champion along the way. Turning to Facebook, I found Flo and the WWRR group. When I learned that the Conga planned to meet in Cheyenne, Wyoming at a time that worked perfectly with my itinerary, I joined the cause. That 2010 Conga was my first; the pictures in this book were taken at the 2011 Conga.

People assume that I'm a cancer survivor because I've ridden some 17,000 miles across the country raising money and awareness for breast cancer causes. I am not a survivor, but when a disease afflicts one in eight women as breast cancer does, everyone knows someone with it, including me.

When I strapped that pink bra across my windshield people instantly knew I was doing something for breast cancer and asked to get their pictures with my bike, which gave me an opportunity to ask for donations and to hear how breast cancer had touched either themselves or the women in their lives.

Nothing could have prepared me for the outpouring I received at rest stops, gas stations and tourist attractions from North Carolina to Oregon and back. I remember one woman in particular who approached me at a rest stop overlooking Lake Bonneville in Utah, carrying a 2-year-old on her hip. She wanted me to know that she had found a lump on her breast when she was 15 years old and survived to become a mother some 12 years later.

Thinking through the stories I heard on the road and from my fellow Conga riders, I came to appreciate the role that a brush with cancer had played in helping survivors re-examine their priorities and assumptions about how to live their best lives. This book is a way for me to share some of the wisdom they've imparted in a way that will help readers apply the lessons to their own lives.

Since the preponderance of survivors I met are women, I feature women in this book. While the lessons can apply to everyone, I can't say whether a book based on men's stories would have differed significantly. Perhaps I'll take that up at another time. Until then, I hope you'll be able to apply the lessons in this book to your life.

WHEN I STRAPPED THAT PINK BRA ACROSS MY WINDSHIELD PEOPLE INSTANTLY KNEW I WAS DOING SOMETHING FOR BREAST CANCER AND ASKED TO GET THEIR PICTURES WITH MY BIKE.

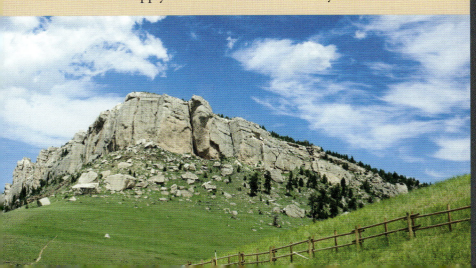

Live Full Throttle

Applying the Lessons

The book's eight chapters each feature a story, photos and exercises to help us access our inner wisdom. Brains need stories; we're biologically wired for them. Psychologists tell us that it's through stories that we can get inside the heads and lives of people whom we've never actually met. The images help us access thoughts and emotions. Please, don't just look at the photos, look into them while recalling the story and lesson of each chapter. I included thought-provoking exercises at the end of each chapter because without them, you run the risk of simply thinking, "oh, that's a nice story," or "wow, that makes sense" and then going on about your day. If you take the time to work them both on paper and in your life, I guarantee you'll see positive changes in how you think, feel and act.

I did not place photos of the women themselves with the chapters they inspired. Rather, I chose photos taken in the Big Sky region and the Conga rally that embody the theme of each chapter. Your left brain may yearn to know which woman did this or that, but your right brain doesn't need such detail to help you absorb the lesson and apply it to your life.

Breathe.

Cancer Inequality?

One final note. People often ask whether breast cancer gets an unfair share of attention and funding. A medical director at an oncology clinic once told me that because breast cancer strikes at the emotional center of our society—women—society is particularly generous to breast cancer causes. Because of this generosity, we know more about it than we do other cancers.

What many people don't realize is that scientists have applied breast cancer findings to other forms of the disease. In other words, a beneficial spillover effect of progress with breast cancer has made life better for us all.

It's time we change our tendency to view things through a competitive lens, a lens that says breast cancer is "competing" unfairly with other cancers for attention and funding.

It's cancer.

IT'S TIME WE CHANGE OUR TENDENCY TO VIEW THINGS THROUGH A COMPETITIVE LENS, A LENS THAT SAYS BREAST CANCER IS "COMPETING" UNFAIRLY WITH OTHER CANCERS FOR ATTENTION AND FUNDING.

IT'S CANCER.

Live Full Throttle

The Eight Lessons

THE HEALING POWER OF *Joy*

Five years after a double mastectomy, Dusty's breast cancer returned as metastatic encapsulated tumors in her lungs. After three unsuccessful rounds of chemotherapy, her medical team encouraged her stay in their care until they could find a clinical trial for her.

Instead, Dusty chose to wring the joy out of whatever life she had left.

It was her daughter's last summer of childhood (she was headed off to college in the fall) and Dusty knew that chemo would exhaust her. She signed out of treatment against medical advice, soaked up time with her daughter and rode her motorcycle from New Mexico to Wyoming with other women raising money and awareness for breast cancer research.

I met her as part of the 2010 Conga and she accompanied me across Colorado to Nebraska as I headed home. Dusty rode with a half helmet and sunglasses, which exposed most of her fair skin to the elements. Taking a break from the mid-day sun at a sandwich shop near the Nebraska state line, I asked if she'd like to use some of my sunscreen and she told me that she'd already slathered her face with it. I was shocked, thinking perhaps it wasn't working. Smiling, she explained that chemo makes many breast cancer patients, including herself, photosensitive. As if anticipating an unasked question she continued with something like, "If the cancer kills me anyway, what's it matter if my corpse has a little sun damage?"

About two months after that afternoon at the sandwich shop, Dusty went back for a checkup to learn that she was inexplicably CANCER FREE. When I told my doctor this story she replied, "Tamela, medical science has not yet learned how to quantify the healing effects of joy."

Undaunted and indomitable Dusty. When she focused on living a joyful life, the healing power of joy rewarded her with a longer life.

WHEN SHE FOCUSED ON LIVING

a joyful life,

THE HEALING POWER OF JOY

REWARDED HER WITH

a longer life.

Exercises

Ask yourself, What can I do today that would fill me with joy? TODAY.

Today I will. . .

Remember a time when something you had been worried
about came to a better conclusion than you envisioned.

How long ago was this?

How did that outcome affect your life today?

How can you apply that experience to a problem you're facing today?

Go back through the images in this chapter and choose the one that looks most "joyful" to you. Ask the subject in that photo for some advice on bringing more joy into your life. For example, what does a wild desert burro know about joy that you don't?

Write that advice down here.

Gratitude
Eases Pain

In 2005 Karen was diagnosed with Choroidal Melanoma, a form of eye cancer, which she described as "a skate" compared to what came five years later. In a three-month period during 2010, her position with an Episcopal parish was terminated and her husband left her.

So what's a laid-off minister facing divorce do with a paid sabbatical between employment and unemployment? Take a motorcycle trip on her Suzuki Boulevard, of course.

But what began as a wind-in-the-face opportunity to assess life and career options ended in an orthopedic exoskeleton from neck to midsection when Karen was literally run over by a Mack truck several states from home.

In a set of cruel parallels, Karen and I returned to Charlotte from our 2010 cross-country motorcycle trips

on the very same day. I wheeled into a celebration with family, friends and two TV crews; Karen arrived on a train, incapacitated and accompanied by her care-giving mother. Karen was an experienced rider who had been riding for three years; I for three months.

Karen is now a Conga "spirit rider," of which there are hundreds. Spirit riders cheer on and pray for those riding the Conga, sometimes hosting them when they come through their towns. I learned about Karen's motorcycle misadventure from a mutual acquaintance, but I was reluctant to meet her because my cross-country trip was triumph to her tragedy. I didn't want to be salt in her motorcycling wound.

My apprehension was unfounded. Karen is no sad sack—she's an inspiration. Listening to her story, the theme of gratitude, not despair, prevailed. When she was unable to take care of even her most basic physical needs, she focused on gratitude: she was grateful to be alive; grateful to the emergency responders and medical professionals; grateful to be taken care of by her mother and friends.

What advice does a woman who's lost her job, her mate and her health give to the rest of us? "Do what's in front of you. Don't get so concerned with what's next that (you) miss the beauty or experience of the present."

Even when what's in front of you is re-learning tasks you'd once mastered as a toddler.

WHAT ADVICE DOES A WOMAN WHO'S LOST

HER JOB,

HER MATE

AND HER HEALTH

GIVE TO THE REST OF US?

Do WHAT'S IN FRONT OF *you.*

"When you leave home
to follow your dreams,
your road will probably
be riddled with potholes,
not always paved in happy
technicolor bricks."
~ Kelly Cutrone (If You
Have To Cry, Go Outside)

Exercises

REMEMBER KAREN'S ADVICE TO "DO WHAT'S IN FRONT OF YOU." WITHOUT LOOKING BACK AT THINGS YOU CAN'T CHANGE, WITHOUT LOOKING FORWARD MORE THAN 24 HOURS, WHAT STEP CAN YOU TAKE TODAY THAT WILL BRING YOU A SENSE OF SATISFACTION OR ACCOMPLISHMENT? TODAY.

Today I will. . .

KAREN SAYS HER EXPERIENCES TAUGHT HER TO GRAB ANY OPPORTUNITY TO NURTURE RELATIONSHIPS. REFERRING TO OPPORTUNITIES SHE MISSED TO SAVE HER MARRIAGE, SHE SAID, "I HAVE A NEW RESOLVE NOT TO BLOW IT NEXT TIME."

WHAT RELATIONSHIP WILL YOU NURTURE TODAY?

HOW WILL YOU NURTURE IT?

Gratitude

"SHOWING GRATITUDE IS ONE OF THE SIMPLEST
YET MOST POWERFUL THINGS HUMANS CAN DO
FOR EACH OTHER." ~ RANDY PAUSCH (THE LAST LECTURE)

IMAGINE YOURSELF SO INCAPACITATED THAT YOU CAN'T EVEN BATHE YOURSELF. WOULD YOU BE GRATEFUL? KAREN SHOWED ME THAT YOU CAN ALWAYS FIND SOMETHING TO BE GRATEFUL FOR.

List five things you are grateful for today.

1.

2.

3.

4.

5.

Laughter LIGHTENS TRAGEDY

After her mastectomy, Debbie sent a series of newsletter updates to friends, co-workers and clients. One announced that "The Uniboober" would be back to work and asked that if anyone noticed the "falsie" down at her waist, would they please let her know so she could put it back where it belonged.

"It's either laugh or cry, and crying takes too much out of you," she explained. Debbie's right. Science has proven that laughing lowers blood pressure; it gives the facial, leg, back, abdominal, respiratory, and diaphragm muscles a good workout and strengthens the immune system.

When I met Debbie during the 2010 Conga in Wyoming, she was in vibrant health. The wattage produced by her toothy smile could illuminate her home state of Texas. Seven months after our Conga encounter, her husband announced on Facebook that cancer had metastasized, rampaging her liver, bones, lymph system, spine, and lungs. Her bones leached marrow into her bloodstream. The Houston medical team said there was nothing they could do for her, but she found a more optimistic hospital outside Chicago.

"There's always an option around the corner. I told my family there would be no more sad faces." They evidently heeded her advice; a series of family photos taken soon after her chemo showed everyone sneaking two-fingered horns over someone else's head.

Debbie told me her story in August of 2011, speaking from her home office, where she sells hazardous waste disposal services. She was her effervescent self, telling me the good news that after several rounds of chemo in Chicago she was again cancer free. On the other hand, like so many chemo patients, the cure had taken its toll on the rest of her. The woman who said "You have to be happy to get through this" was in the hospital some six hours later fighting liver failure. Probably with laughter.

YOU HAVE TO BE HAPPY TO GET THROUGH THIS.

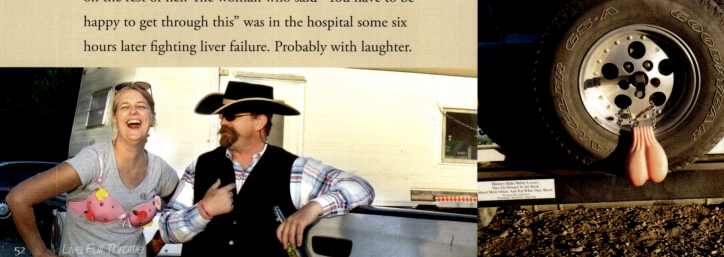

IT'S EITHER
LAUGH OR
CRY, AND
CRYING TAKES
TOO MUCH
OUT OF YOU.

Exercises

THE OPPOSITE OF GRIEF IS ECSTASY. THE OPPOSITE OF SADNESS IS JOY. HUMANS ARE SUCH COMPLEX BEINGS THAT WE CAN ALTERNATE BETWEEN OPPOSITE EMOTIONS INSTANTLY AND SOMETIMES FEEL BOTH SIMULTANEOUSLY, LIKE A SWEET AND SOUR CANDY.

THERE'S A THEATER/FILM GENRE CALLED THE "TRAGICOMEDY." FILMS LIKE *FARGO*, *LIFE IS BEAUTIFUL* AND *ONE FLEW OVER THE CUCKOO'S NEST* ARE FILMS YOU MAY HAVE ALREADY ENJOYED. IF YOU HAVEN'T SEEN ANY OF THESE, AND CAN'T THINK OF A TRAGICOMEDY YOU MIGHT HAVE SEEN, GO TO WWW.FLICKCHART.COM AND SEARCH THROUGH THEIR LIST OF 50 TRAGICOMEDIES...SURELY ONE WILL CAPTURE YOUR INTEREST. WATCH A TRAGICOMEDY AND RELATE A SCENE OR TWO TO YOUR LIFE.

MOVIE:

SCENE:

I LAUGHED AT:

I WINCED AT:

HOW THE SCENE RELATES TO MY LIFE:

THINK OF SOMETHING IN YOUR LIFE THAT ISN'T GOING AS YOU'D HOPED OR EXPECTED. PERHAPS IT'S A DOWNRIGHT TRAGEDY. PUT YOURSELF IN THE POSITION OF A GENIUS STORYTELLER AND FIND SOMETHING FUNNY IN THE SITUATION. C'MON, YOU CAN DO IT—JUST LIKE THE TIME YOU LAUGHED DURING A FUNERAL OR A DRESSING DOWN BY THE SCHOOL PRINCIPAL.

Write the funny part here ⟶

YOU MIGHT NEED TO PRACTICE LAUGHING. LOOK UP LAUGHTER YOGA OR LAUGHTER CLUBS IN YOUR AREA OR HIT WWW.LAUGHTERYOGA.ORG FOR VIDEOS AND INFORMATION THAT WILL GET YOU IN THE LAUGHTER GROOVE.

You're Terminal Too, *Embrace* It

When I tell you that Karen is a former ski school instructor, seasonal game butcher and firefighter, I bet your mental picture doesn't conjure a little wisp of a thing, which she is. This granola girl eats healthy foods, rarely drinks alcohol, doesn't smoke and has never, to her knowledge, been exposed to the pesticides and industrial chemicals that are usually associated with her specific type of lymphoma.

"If you live right, there's an assumption that you'll live a long and healthy life" says Karen, who was diagnosed at age 47. "My cancer diagnosis was the ultimate 'shit happens experience.'"

Given an eight-year prognosis, Karen says that while you can rail against it, pout, whine, deny, and

I'M NO DIFFERENT
THAN ANYONE ELSE,

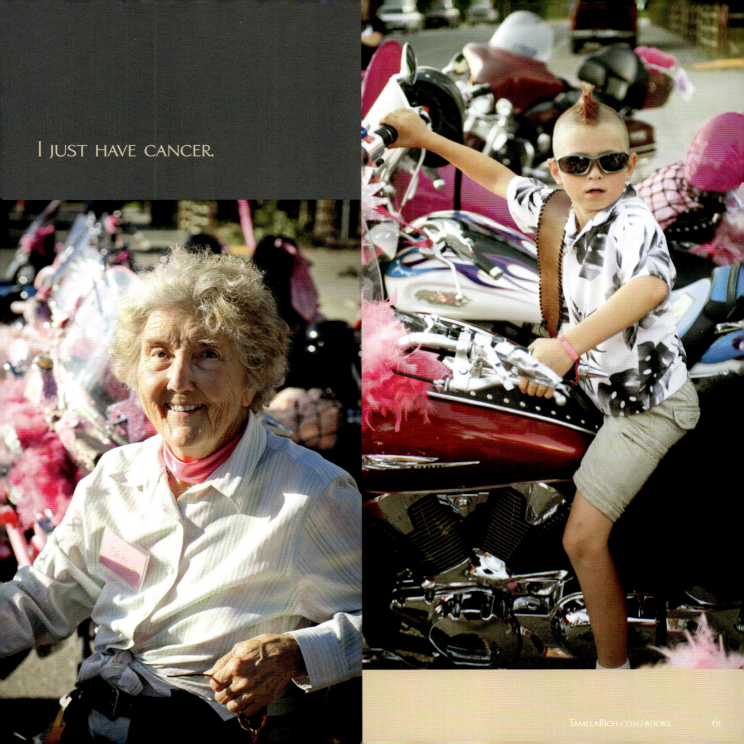

I JUST HAVE CANCER.

try every new treatment, the real choice is whether you face cancer as a victim or a survivor. In the words of a true Pacific Northwesterner she resolved, "I'm not dead yet; I'm going to pilot this." She doesn't tell people she's sick, "I'm no different than anyone else, I just have cancer."

Karen had always wanted to learn how to drive a motorcycle but put it off because she was afraid she'd really love it and would therefore have to "do something about it." She was right. I met her during our 2010 Conga, when she had been riding just a little over a year. By the time we met again in 2011 she was one of very few to pass a grueling motorcycle course designed by law enforcement officers to help civilians drive like cops.

She describes herself as a "real" biker now. The granola girl who rides like a cop doesn't think twice about her appearance when arriving at a destination spackled with road grime. "Because of the bike I'm more willing to be myself, which is rewarding because I'm told, not just by bikers, that I've never looked better and I've never looked or felt more confident."

This new-found confidence enabled her to deliver a difficult "I message" to a family member who expected her to comfort him in his grief over her diagnosis, instead of the opposite way around. She honestly told him, "I can't emotionally support you. I'm the patient here."

I'M MORE WILLING TO BE MYSELF.

Exercises

Karen took stock in her relationships and made some changes in the ones that weren't working for her. She gave some people very specific instructions for how she wished to be treated.

What ONE person in your life do you wish would change the way they relate to you?

Embrace

How can you describe the change you want to see in this relationship? For example, "Instead of (this behavior), I want to see (that behavior)."

Replace "this behavior" and "that behavior" with words of your own. *Write them here, right now.*

How long are you willing to wait for the unhealthy relationship to change? What action will you take if it doesn't change by that time?

"Conformity is the jailer of freedom and the enemy of growth." ~ John F. Kennedy

It took a cancer diagnosis for Karen to decide to indulge her motorcycle fantasy. What three things would you do with your life if you had eight more years to live? What if it were eight more weeks? It could very well be eight more hours—none of us know.

1.

2.

3.

Choose one of the three. What baby step can you take TODAY to launch that dream? Is it looking up a training class? Roughing out a budget? Asking a friend for help? *Write that step down here.*

Live Full Throttle

WHEN TO *Fight*
WHEN TO *Flow*

After her double mastectomy, when she took that first look in the mirror, Gussie recalls breaking down. Her husband reassured her. She said to him, "I know, just give me this moment to grieve and I'll be okay. This is not going to rule me."

Chemotherapy drugs indiscriminately attack all new cells, including hair follicles—which is why most patients lose their hair. But hair is more easily forfeited and approximated than a breast. Gussie endured five reconstructive surgeries and told me in her Alabama drawl, "If I'd known how hard it was going to be to get new boobs, I would have said forget it." But when Gussie looks in the mirror now, she doesn't see the scars; she sees her breasts.

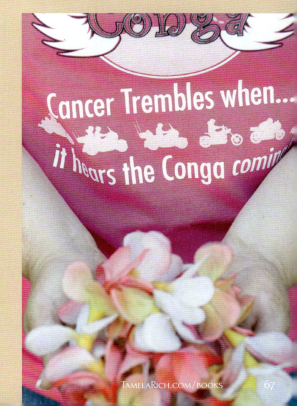

Breast cancer and surgeries taught her how to fight. "It reared up a fight in me that I didn't know I had. I never realized I could be so strong. I'm like a bulldog," she says, Steel Magnolia style.

Her travails also taught her to flow. Gussie says the little things that used to really upset her just don't bother her now, including admitting her age. "I love life and I love celebrating each birthday." Before her cancer, she re-celebrated her 39th birthday, now she admits to celebrating over 50 of them.

Gussie is also able to flow with the big things in life. When we talked poolside at the Yellowstone Inn in Greybull, where the big Wyoming skies were un-puncutated by clouds, she and her husband were enjoying an unprecedented three-week vacation. Without her telling me so, I wouldn't have known by her demeanor that back home in Alabama her father was in the hospital and another family member was incarcerated, awaiting trial. "If it's something you can't control, just let it go," she sighed, shrugging. "If you can't control it, it's just a thing."

If it's something you can't control, just let it go.

THIS

IS NOT

GOING

TO

RULE

ME.

Exercises

Take a long look at this photo of melting glacial snow on a mountain face. This scene captures the interplay of water, wood and earth, and is a metaphor for harnessing the power of emotions.

First, observe the two states of water—the liquid and the solid. Think about your emotions as you look at these two states of water. Water is fluid or solid according to temperature, while human emotions are influenced by thoughts and beliefs.

Do your emotions usually flow or freeze?

Think about a time when you should have been still, like ice, but instead, you ran, like water.

Now consider a time when you should have been flexible, looking for the easiest path to your destination, but instead, stayed stuck.

"Until you find something to fight for, you settle for something to fight against." ~ Chuck Palahniuk

Wood grows, expands, nourishes and rests and does so at the appropriate times. We can learn from wood's wisdom.

How do you know if you are out of balance? Ask yourself: are you nourishing others at the expense of personal expansion? Or perhaps by growing while sacrificing rest?

What should you be doing now? Growing, expanding, nourishing or resting?

Flow

WE THINK OF MOUNTAINS AS FORCEFUL, STRONG AND UNYIELDING, YET HERE WE SEE THE MOUNTAIN FACE BEING SHAPED BY BOTH THE WATER AND THE WOOD.

WHAT EXTERNAL FORCES ARE SHAPING YOU?

ARE THEY SHAPING YOU APPROPRIATELY?

UNLIKE A MOUNTAIN, YOU CAN MOVE AWAY FROM UNPRODUCTIVE FORCES. WHAT THING IN YOUR LIFE WILL YOU MOVE AWAY FROM STARTING RIGHT NOW? *Write that here.*

GUSSIE LEARNED TO SPEND HER ENERGY ON THE THINGS IN LIFE THAT MATTER. WHAT ARE TWO THINGS YOU'VE BEEN GIVING YOUR ENERGY TO, EVEN IN SMALL INCREMENTS, THAT CANNOT BENEFIT FROM YOUR OBSESSION? IS IT SOMETHING POLITICAL? PERHAPS IT'S THE HEALTH OF A LOVED ONE. OR MAYBE SOME HOME REPAIRS OR REMODELING YOU CAN'T AFFORD RIGHT NOW. *Write those two things here.*

1.

2.

Flow

IF YOU CAN'T CONTROL IT,

IT'S JUST A THING. ~ GUSSIE

WRITE DOWN TWO THINGS THAT YOU CAN DO SOMETHING ABOUT, BUT THAT YOU HAVEN'T TAKEN ACTION ON.

1.

2.

REPEAT AFTER ME, "THE ENERGY I'VE BEEN SPENDING ON THE FIRST TWO THINGS WILL BE CHANNELED TO THE SECOND TWO THINGS."

THE NEXT TIME ONE OF THE FIRST TWO THINGS TAKES ROOT IN YOUR HEAD, GENTLY REPLACE IT WITH ONE OF THE SECOND TWO THINGS.

You can do it.

Art RESTORES

Deb had been hand quilting for over 20 years before her breast cancer diagnosis and enjoyed gifting her creations. She averaged two baby quilts or a full-sized bedspread every year, progressing from simple squares to intricate patterns over time. But she shut down during her cancer treatments and the reconstructive process, telling herself she didn't have time to indulge her passion while managing her recovery.

Her daily journaling practice lapsed before the diagnosis and she tried to start again as a way to cope. She soon found her pages full of negative thoughts and feelings, so she gave that up as well.

Her sister-in-law Mary called one day with a commission to make a quilt for her best friend,

Denise, who needed something to snuggle with after her back surgery. "I think Mary KNEW I needed something to keep my mind off cancer," said Deb.

Mary also suggested that Deb begin journaling again, but, with a twist, she could talk about her quilting process and how it made her feel. "So I basically jotted down my thoughts...how I was feeling each time I worked on the piece, the weather, or something about the area I was working on, and how I felt AFTER working on it."

"ONE GOOD THING ABOUT MUSIC, WHEN IT HITS YOU, YOU FEEL NO PAIN."
~ BOB MARLEY

Looking back, Deb observed that time spent quilting produced some sort of "high" that eased her physical and emotional pain. "I truly think the simplicity of the stitches and the rhythm of the hand work was therapeutic for me. My mind was freed from the worry, stress and pain through the beauty of the colors and the mind-hand connection."

Denise's quilt was crafted entirely by hand and took Deb more than a thousand hours over the course of a year, start to finish. Deb didn't intend to give Denise the quilt journal, but when she shared it with Mary, they agreed that the journal was integral to the quilt. Deb and Denise met for the first time when the quilt was finished and had a good cry.

"I love the idea that I give of myself to others when I make something. It's like giving someone a HUG they can wrap themselves up in any time it's needed!"

"THE GREAT
CREATOR HAS
GIFTED US
WITH CREATIVITY.

OUR GIFT BACK IS
OUR USE OF IT."

~ JULIA CAMERON
(THE ARTIST'S WAY)

Exercises

DEB ORIGINALLY THOUGHT OF QUILTING AS AN INDULGENCE. SHE USED HER CREATIVITY TO HELP HEAL SOMEONE ELSE, THEN REALIZED HOW THERAPEUTIC IT WAS FOR HERSELF. WHAT CREATIVE THINGS DO YOU ENJOY? POPSICLE STICK SCULPTURES? HUMMING THROUGH A KAZOO? POETRY? KARAOKE? WRITE ALL OF THEM DOWN HERE.

WHAT CREATIVE THINGS HAVE YOU EVER GIVEN UP AND WHY?

THIS BOOK IS FULL OF CREATIVE IMAGES. DECORATED BRAS ON BIKES, CHESTS, HEADS AND TREES. DJS WEARING BRAS. PEOPLE OF ALL AGES ENJOYING A LITTLE BIT OF PLAY ACTING AND MERRIMENT. GO BACK THROUGH THE IMAGES IN THE ENTIRE BOOK, THEN WRITE DOWN WHAT COMES TO MIND ABOUT YOUR OWN CREATIVE PROCESS. SHOULD YOU BE SILLIER IN YOUR CREATIVE PROCESS OR PROJECTS? SHOULD YOU INCLUDE OTHERS IN YOUR CREATIVE PROCESS OR GIVE MORE OF YOUR CREATIVE PROJECTS AWAY?

"THERE IS A VITALITY, A LIFE FORCE, AN ENERGY, A QUICKENING THAT IS TRANSLATED THROUGH YOU INTO ACTION, AND BECAUSE THERE IS ONLY ONE OF YOU IN ALL TIME, THIS EXPRESSION IS UNIQUE. AND IF YOU BLOCK IT, IT WILL NEVER EXIST THROUGH ANY OTHER MEDIUM AND WILL BE LOST." ~ MARTHA GRAHAM

Pablo Picasso said, "Only put off until tomorrow what you are willing to die having left undone." Is your creativity flowing or blocked? If it is blocked, don't waste time wondering why. Take action right now by connecting these dots in an interesting way and while you're doing so, hum a little ditty you learned in elementary school.

```
        *                       *                   * *

    *     *                   * *                   *       *

            *           *               *                 * *

        *   *   *           *   *           *   *       *       *               *
```

Write your commitment to YOUR creative process right now, so you don't weasel out of it.

Live Full Throttle

Relationships
ARE FLUID

When a person gets a cancer diagnosis, that person, the family, and in some cases an extended circle of people, is given an opportunity to re-evaluate their priorities, their relationships and their lives.

One story I heard, as I collected these vignettes, involved an entire branch office pooling their sick days so that a co-worker with cancer could continue being paid during her surgery, chemo, radiation and recovery.

More than one woman I talked to had either hidden her diagnosis or minimized it to her children. One in particular felt so out of control of her life that it seemed to me that managing her health information was all she had left. Another woman lied to her children about her cancer re-occurring, telling them she was shaving her head in solidarity with a friend instead of admitting she was back in chemo. When her children learned the truth it had a devastating effect on their relationship. "Your child knows if they can't trust you. If a relationship is built on lies it won't matter what you say anyway."

I know women with cancer in loveless marriages who stay for financial reasons, including health insurance.

One woman saw in retrospect that her marriage was over well before her cancer diagnosis. She came to see that her husband had the grace to stick with her until she was years into remission. This took the usual rancor out of their divorce proceedings.

Several women told me that their marriages were stronger after the cancer because it focused the couple's attention on each other's merits or because it brought out the nurturing side of their mates.

While no two relationships changed in the same way, cancer was a catalyst that drew some people closer and forced others further apart. Several said they saw cancer as a blessing in disguise, causing them to take stock in relationships they had taken for granted and to make necessary changes. Regardless of whether a relationship brings us joy or sorrow, each relationship gives us the opportunity to grow stronger, nobler and more compassionate with ourselves and others.

CANCER WAS A CATALYST THAT DREW SOME PEOPLE CLOSER AND FORCED OTHERS FURTHER APART.

"Let there be spaces in your togetherness, and let the winds of the heavens dance between you. Love one another but make

not a bond of love: Let it rather be a moving sea between the shores of your souls. Fill each other's cup but drink not from one cup. Give one another of your bread but eat not from the same loaf.

Sing and dance together and be joyous, but let each one of you be alone, Even as the strings of a lute are alone though they quiver with the same music. Give your hearts, but not into each other's keeping. For only the hand of Life can contain your hearts. And stand together, yet not too near together: For the pillars of the temple stand apart, And the oak tree and the cypress grow not in each other's shadow."

~ Khalil Gibran (The Prophet)

Exercises

JUST TAKE A MINUTE TO THINK ABOUT SOMEONE WITH WHOM YOU HAD A CHERISHED RELATIONSHIP WHO'S NO LONGER LIVING. YOUR PARENT? A SIBLING? A TEACHER? WRITE THEIR NAME HERE AND A SENTENCE OR TWO ABOUT THE NATURE OF THE RELATIONSHIP.

WHAT ADVICE WOULD THAT PERSON GIVE YOU ON HOW TO FIX OR ENHANCE A KEY RELATIONSHIP WITH SOMEONE STILL LIVING? WRITE THAT ADVICE DOWN HERE.

"I MEAN, IF THE RELATIONSHIP CAN'T SURVIVE THE LONG TERM, WHY ON EARTH WOULD IT BE WORTH MY TIME AND ENERGY FOR THE SHORT TERM?" ~ NICHOLAS SPARKS (THE LAST SONG)

WHAT RELATIONSHIP IN YOUR LIFE HAS NO LONG-TERM CHANCE FOR SURVIVAL BASED ON HOW IT'S GOING NOW?

ARE YOU WILLING TO DO YOUR PART TO PUT IT ON THE RIGHT PATH? WHAT WOULD THAT ENTAIL?

IS IT CRUEL OR KIND TO END THE RELATIONSHIP SOONER THAN LATER?

"DEATH ENDS A LIFE, NOT A RELATIONSHIP."

~ MITCH ALBOM (TUESDAYS WITH MORRIE)

"INDIFFERENCE AND NEGLECT OFTEN DO MUCH
MORE DAMAGE THAN OUTRIGHT DISLIKE."
~ J.K. ROWLING
(HARRY POTTER AND THE
ORDER OF THE PHOENIX)

WHAT RELATIONSHIP NEEDS SOME TENDER LOVING
CARE? DON'T SPEND TIME BEATING YOURSELF UP
FOR NEGLECTING IT. DO SOMETHING ABOUT IT.
Right Now.

WHAT ONE THING CAN YOU DO TODAY TO
DEMONSTRATE YOUR LOVE OR APPRECIATION TO
SOMEONE WHO NEEDS A LIFT? *Do It.*

"WHEN YOU ARE IN THE FINAL DAYS OF YOUR LIFE,
WHAT WILL YOU WANT? WILL YOU HUG THAT
COLLEGE DEGREE IN THE WALNUT FRAME? WILL
YOU ASK TO BE CARRIED TO THE GARAGE SO YOU
CAN SIT IN YOUR CAR? WILL YOU FIND COMFORT
IN REREADING YOUR FINANCIAL STATEMENT? OF
COURSE NOT. WHAT WILL MATTER THEN WILL BE
PEOPLE. IF RELATIONSHIPS WILL MATTER MOST THEN,
SHOULDN'T THEY MATTER MOST NOW?"
~ MAX LUCADO

Relationships

Channel Sorrow
into *Service*

With a nod to the affects cancer has on family, friends and the world, consider what Flo did when she faced cancer with her beloved sister, Janet.

Flo and Janet grew up in Alberta and British Columbia, (Canada, for the geography-challenged among us), part of a rambunctious family of nine children in which the older kids helped raise the younger. All the siblings admit that Janet was their favorite. Flo describes Janet as the motherly type who always had it together, a gentle soul who apparently had colon cancer a couple of years before it was diagnosed.

Flo says she remembers sitting bedside with her 40-year-old sister and saying, "You know Janet, I would die for you right now, so why are you dying first?" Janet said she thought maybe God was taking her first to make it easier on everyone when the next one passed.

After Janet's death in 1996, Flo wanted to do something in her memory, aspiring to perhaps dedicate a plaque in the hallway of a hospital. Now look at what Flo has accomplished in Janet's name. The Conga ride she started in 2008 raised $1700, then $12,000 in 2009. Counting 2011's success, the group has raised over $90,000. That's a lot of hospital plaques.

Although fundraising is easier to tally than lives changed, it is but one measure of impact. People from across North America—and not just motorcyclists—reach out to Flo in their journeys with cancer, whether to cry on her shoulder or celebrate a clean test result. Many of them will never meet Flo in person, but they feel they know her from the tireless cheerleading she does in her blog and from Facebook. I believe she answers every email, every social media poke and every comment.

I guess all those years in a big family prepared her to extend her loving arms to the rest of the world, including

I WOULD DIE FOR YOU RIGHT NOW,

WHY ARE YOU DYING FIRST?

me. When I planned my first cross-country trip, people responded anywhere from "You go, girl," to "You'll kill yourself." Most people who knew anything about motorcycling tried to talk me out of my adventure because I'd only been riding three months and therefore I didn't know what I didn't know. Flo encouraged me through several phone calls, and also warned me of the importance of checking over my shoulder before making lane changes. This advice saved me from several unhappy encounters with cars in my blind spot. I still think of her every time I do a "shoulder check."

Thanks, Flo.

Exercises

Go back to the opening page of this chapter and look at the picture of the bees working in the cactus flowers. Bees are tiny creatures, yet without them, agriculture would cease and we would starve. Remember the bees when you are feeling insignificant. Remember what Flo did by combining her passion for motorcycling with her desire to, in her words, "kick cancer to the curb." What can you do in your own little corner of the world? Can you pray? Start there. Make a commitment right here to do something that makes a difference.

In the Relationships are Fluid chapter, I asked you to remember someone with whom you had a cherished relationship who's no longer living. Bring that person back to mind now by writing their name and a sentence about what they meant to your life here.

"Every time you do a good deed you shine the light a little farther into the dark. And the thing is, when you're gone that light is going to keep shining on, pushing the shadows back." ~ Charles de Lint

Now, honor that person's memory through an act of service. What will that service be? Did they have a favorite cause that you can help with a donation of time or talent?

If money and time were no object, what cause(s) would you align with? Write down the issues that are meaningful to you.

Maybe you're housebound or on a tight budget. You can serve with a kindly word. Flo spends a lot of time encouraging people via email, her blog and Facebook. What tiny light can you flash in a dark corner of your world? No act of service is insignificant.

Service

Live Full Throttle

Afterword

The night before returning to Charlotte, North Carolina, from my first Conga ride in 2010, I rendezvoused with four motorcycling friends in Asheville, a Blue Ridge Mountain town a couple of hours away. My four friends had witnessed me wiping out in a rainstorm three months earlier on a rented bike, and although they worried about my safety on the 18-state journey from North Carolina to Oregon and back, they cheered me on and helped me prepare. Returning unscathed to their enthusiastic embraces and high fives was my first emotional victory lap.

I knew that there would be TV crews and a newspaper reporter or two waiting to talk to me the next day at my welcome-home party, but had no idea how I would respond to the inevitable question of why I did it. Why had I done it? Yes, I needed to work on the book project in Oregon, but I could have

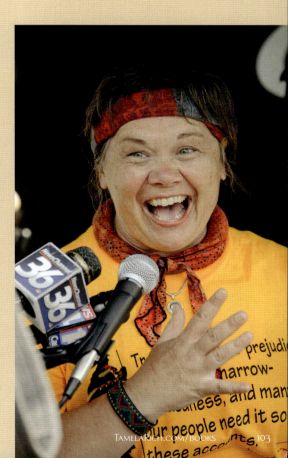

easily flown there and back, so that wasn't it. Why had I decided to set off on a mostly-solo trek with so little preparation? I listened to my answers carefully that night as my friends asked me about my experience, but I went to bed without the wished for "aha" moment of clarity.

The bikers planned a great route home through a few stretches of twisty roads between Asheville and Lake Lure. Ask any experienced motorcyclist and they'll tell you how much they enjoy a nice twisty road; ask any inexperienced biker about riding twisties and watch the color drain from their face. I rode in "the cradle" that day—my term for being in the middle of the line of bikes—and when we stopped for breakfast in Lake Lure my friends remarked that my skills were much improved

WHY HAD I DECIDED TO SET OFF ON A MOSTLY-SOLO TREK WITH SO LITTLE PREPARATION?

after 7500 miles behind me; I could feel it myself, too. But something emotional was welling up alongside the pride over my technical skills. What was it?

Our next stop was the Bantam Chef diner in Chesnee, South Carolina, chockablock with 1950s memorabilia including a 1950 restored Studebaker and a 1958 BMW Isetta. You can smell its cooking oil from a block away on a normal day, and from three blocks away on a summer day when the air doesn't move. August 8, 2010 was a three-block day.

I love diners, dives and greasy spoons, especially when the kitsch on the walls is collected, not manufactured, and the owners themselves refill your ice tea from a pitcher. No one else in my family quite appreciates these establishments as I do, which made me reflect on the

freedom I'd enjoyed on my trip to eat where I wanted to, and with whom I wanted. How I had lingered over interesting conversations with patrons and wait staff and had been able to tell them anything I wanted about myself. Heck, I could have even lied about who I was and what I was doing if I'd wanted to.

During that last hour on the bike, nearing the re-entry zone of my former life, I thought about identity, my identity, and the identity that others ascribed to me. I thought about the person that my fellow Conga riders knew me to be. She was different in many key ways from the person that my closest friends and family had come to know over a longer period of time. The Conga rider was a successful adventurer. She had taken a risk that most people had warned her against, and prevailed. She had done something that many middle-aged women dreamed of, sometimes secretly. Most importantly, she had changed the way she thought of herself.

Wheeling into my welcome-home party at Caribou Coffee where family, friends, the anticipated TV news crews and a Charlotte Observer reporter bore witness to my accomplishment, I was indeed asked why I did it. I heard myself say that I'd had a lot of failures in my life and this trip was a way for me to redefine myself as a success. Funny, it only became clear to me why I'd done it after it was done.

From Failed Business Owner to Successful Human Being

Rewind four years from that first Conga ride and I'd have described myself as the owner and guarantor of a bankrupt business. Facing weekly capital calls from friends and family who had bankrolled the endeavor, I had taken a calculated risk and failed miserably, taking down with me people who had entrusted their money to my business acumen. My bank account had been swept clean by the Internal Revenue Service. There was no way we could afford college tuition for our children.

Suicide began seducing me long before I got the urge to take action. Mental health professionals call it "suicidal ideation" when that little voice says, "Take a hard left into the oncoming lane and all this shit will go away." If that little voice has been speaking to you, too, get help immediately.

One day I snapped. Not in the sense of falling into a heap; what I fell into was a sort of trance. Driving home from another day of taking creditor and investor calls and dealing with a

I HAD TAKEN A CALCULATED RISK AND FAILED MISERABLY,

workforce that couldn't pass a drug test, the idea persisted that there was one solution that would make everyone happy. If I were dead I wouldn't have to deal with my bungled life and my loved ones would have at least some of their money back from the life insurance proceeds. You're probably saying "but a life insurance policy won't pay on suicide." As a former insurance executive I knew my particular policy would.

Up in my bedroom, I powered up Word on my laptop and directed my spouse in how I wanted him to allocate the proceeds of the policy. There was no "goodbye, cruel world" language; I was entering a unilateral business transaction. My life for the insurance money.

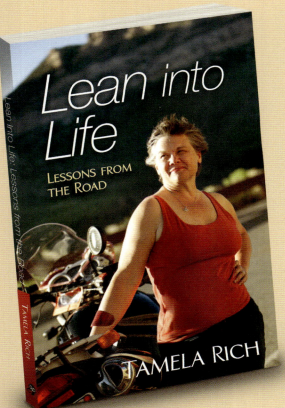

Note finished, I surveyed the meager pharmaceutical contents of my medicine cabinet, looking up each online, trying to find a lethal combination. With the realization that laxatives, decongestants and analgesics wouldn't do the job, and that something more painful and messy was in order, I started coming out of my trance. My family trickled in from work and school. Someone had to make dinner. Life went on and soon the gravity of what I'd almost done led me to seek medical, psychological and spiritual caregiving. But it took a cross-country motorcycle trip to bring back my mojo.

An Invitation to Lean Into Life

Motorcycling gave me a new metaphor for exploring the road of my life, including these insights:

- **Everything wobbles:** Avoiding and recovering from the inevitable spills of life.
- **Blind corners abound:** Ride your best ride and take uncertainty as it comes.
- **Explore the detours:** They're usually providential.
- **Embrace the switchbacks:** The safest way to the mountaintop isn't the shortest.

I invite you to learn more about my story in the forthcoming memoir, *Lean Into Life: Lessons from the Road.* I've never seen a story told in a 356-day series, which I do in *Lean Into Life,* but the format makes sense to me based on my morning ritual: a bit of yoga, inspirational readings and quite prayer and reflection.

I hope you'll give yourself two or three minutes each day to traverse the highways and byways of life with me. Turn the page for two daily samples from *Lean Into Life: Lessons from the Road.*

For books I've written visit **TamelaRich.com/books**.

Tamela Speaks...

to community groups and businesses on the themes of rebirth and transformation from a motorcyclist's perspective.

She invites you along for the ride from the comfort of a conference room chair, at a corporate, social or religious retreat, or in any setting that finds people ready to absorb, be inspired and come away motivated to make an impact in and through their own lives.

Get started by emailing: speaking@tamelarich.com

IT TOOK A CROSS-COUNTRY MOTORCYCLE TRIP

TO BRING BACK MY MOJO.

ASK FOR HELP

I think there's a place for lone wolfing, bootstrapping and self-reliance, but Americans place too much emphasis on rugged individualism. Asking for help shouldn't bring you shame and it might just pay off for all concerned. Know how I got my BMW motorcycle and the training I needed to traverse eighteen states on my 2010 Conga? By asking.

When I asked the BMW Performance Center to sponsor me with a bike and training, I knew it was a long shot. I knew that women are the fastest-growing segment of the motorcycle industry and that BMW motorcycle buyers are typically college educated, working in a managerial or professional role and middle-aged (in other words, women just like me). I figured that my proposition would be fodder for BMW's public relations team if I brought myself and the bike back in one piece, but during the middle of a recession, asking for sponsorship was a crap shoot.

From BMW's perspective, however, they could have spent hundreds of thousands of dollars trying to find a middle-aged woman who'd agree to go on a cross-country motorcycle trip after a couple of days training, and here I landed on their doorstep on my own steam. No wonder they didn't hesitate to say "yes."

There are only two answers to any request—"yes" or "no."
If you never ask the question, the answer's a definite "no."

ONE DAY AT A TIME

Everyone I knew, even those who wished me well and cheered me on, worried that I was taking on an overly ambitious project—7500 miles with about 1000 miles of "seat time" before departure. They worried about lots of things, not only the number of miles, but the weather, the strangers and the animals I would encounter, my lack of mechanical skills and the fact that I'd never traveled that far alone in a car with GPS, much less a motorcycle without it. Looking at it rationally, they were right. But I knew I could do it.

To those who brought up the chicken and egg argument about not having enough seat time to try this cross-country feat, I told them that I was going to take the trip one day at a time. The first day that I rode solo I said, "Today I'm going to drive 275 miles from Cincinnati, Ohio to Valparaiso, Indiana all by myself. I'll stop when I need to stop and deal with whatever comes my way as best I can. It's going to be fun and I'm going to be a better rider by the time I get to Valpo." Sure enough, it was true.

Don't overwhelm yourself thinking about the future.
Do what you must do today to the best of your ability,
with focus and a joyful heart. And do the same tomorrow.

PHOTO CREDITS

Christina Shook was more than the photographer of record for this book. She was a collaborator. Having published her first book, *Chicks on Bikes*, a couple of years before we met, she had great advice on the entire publishing and book marketing process. I'm grateful for her artistic sensibilities and the friendship we forged through working on this project. I look forward to many more opportunities to work together over the course of our careers.

Additional photos supplied by these generous photographers:

- **Catherine Anderson,** page 78 (bra with buttons)
- **Andy Ciordia,** pages 102-107
- **Tannis "Flo" Fuhr,** page 94 (helmet)
- **Dusty Price,** page 36, 85 (burros)
- **Tamela Rich,** pages 6, 26, 30, 40, 69, 73, 75, 92, 93 (landscapes) and 52, 62 (people)

Andy
Catherine
Christina
Dusty
Flo
Tamela